Stand Up for Yourself & Your Friends

Dealing with Bullies and Bossiness, and Finding a Better Way

by Patti Kelley Criswell
illustrated by Angela Martini

American Girl®

Published by American Girl Publishing, Inc.

Copyright © 2009 by American Girl, LLC

Questions or comments? Call 1-800-845-0005,
visit our Web site at **americangirl.com**,
or write to Customer Service, American Girl, 8400 Fairway Place, Middleton, WI 53562-0497.

Printed in China

10 11 12 13 14 15 16 LEO 15 14 13 12 11 10 9 8

Editorial Development: Erin Falligant, Michelle Watkins

Art Direction & Design: Chris Lorette David

Production: Julie Kimmell, Gretchen Krause, Jeannette Bailey, Judith Lary

Illustrations: Angela Martini

Special thanks to The Ophelia Project

Dear Reader,

No matter who you are, it's hard to get along with everyone all the time. There will always be people who challenge you, whether it's an **on-again, off-again friend** or a classmate who's teasing you. Being bullied can feel downright **hurtful,** and when it's happening to you, it's hard to know what to do.

There's no one right way to handle bullying. That's why this book gives you lots of tips to try, such as **clever comebacks, ways to ignore** someone who bullies, and **ways to get help** from an adult you trust. You'll find **advice from girls** who have been there, and you'll learn how to stand up for other people, too, when they need it most.

We can all do our part to make the world a kinder, safer place. After reading this book, you'll know that one person can make a difference—and that person might just be **YOU.**

 Your friends at American Girl

What's Bullying?

Teasing. Taunting. Being mean. No matter what you call it, one thing is for sure: it's all about power. People who bully are trying to take your power—the strong, smart, confident part of you. They're hurting your feelings over and over with actions or words that are *meant* to be hurtful.

aggression   harassment

taunting

teasing   cruelty

5

Is This Bullying?

Think you know what bullying is? Read about each situation, and decide whether or not it's bullying. Circle your choice.

1. A boy in your class was sick and didn't make it to the bathroom in time. Now the kids call him a mean name. You don't call him that, but you laugh along.

   Yes, it's bullying.   No, it's not.

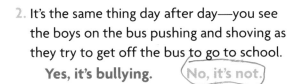

2. It's the same thing day after day—you see the boys on the bus pushing and shoving as they try to get off the bus to go to school.

   Yes, it's bullying.   No, it's not.

3. There is a girl in your class who is different. Lately people have been writing terrible things about her on the computer, but they never say anything to her face.

Yes, it's bullying.   No, it's not.

4. A girl comes up to you in the lunchroom and says, "I don't mean to be rude, but you need to move. Only my friends sit here."

Yes, it's bullying.   No, it's not.

5. One day she's your friend, and the next day she's sitting with someone else and won't talk to you.

Yes, it's bullying.   No, it's not.

6. A girl asks, "Can I play with you guys?" One of your friends says, "Sorry, it's not going to work out today."

Yes, it's bullying.   No, it's not.

7. You sometimes stumble over words when you read aloud. The same girl always corrects you and says, "You don't know that?"

Yes, it's bullying.   No, it's not.

8. You said something kind of mean to a classmate about his mom's car. You apologized afterward and tried to be extra nice to him the rest of the day.

Yes, it's bullying.   No, it's not.

Answers

1. **Yes.** Joining in the laughter means joining in the bullying. In fact, by encouraging the bullying, you may be doing as much harm as the bullies themselves.

2. **Maybe.** Are these boys horsing around playfully, or Is one or more of them trying to hurt or scare the others? Unwanted touching is absolutely bullying. In a situation like this, talk to the bus driver or another trusted adult.

3. **Absolutely.** Gossiping—or talking behind someone's back—is one of the most hurtful forms of bullying. Using the Internet or cell phones to bully is called *cyberbullying,* and it's never O.K.

4. **Yes.** Saying "I don't mean to be rude" or "no offense" doesn't excuse bossy behavior. This girl may think she's a leader, but bossing people around isn't leading—it's bullying.

5. **Yes.** Being an on-again, off-again friend is bullying. If you've tried to talk to her and the bullying keeps happening, you two may need a break. Let your friend know that you need space, but be polite when you see her.

6. **Maybe.** If someone has been treating you and your friends badly, you don't have to play with her. But if your friend is leaving this girl out to make her feel bad, then yes, that's bullying.

7. **It depends.** While this girl may be bragging about her own reading ability, she is embarrassing you in the process. Ask her to please stop. If she doesn't, then yes—it's absolutely bullying.

8. **No.** We all say stupid things once in a while. You let this boy know that you were sorry. It happened once and you did your best to make it right. It was a mistake, not bullying.

What Does a Bully Look Like?

Bullies aren't all rough-and-tough looking. They can be girls or boys, kids or adults. Anyone can bully, even you. In fact, at one time or another, many of us will bully someone else. But whether we're teasing a sibling or leaving out a friend, it's not O.K.—ever. Here are more examples of bullying:

Gossiping or spreading rumors:
"Psst, did you hear about . . . ?"

Pushing and shoving:
"Move!"

Name-calling:
"She's such a loser."

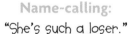

Telling secrets:
"Don't tell her I told you, but . . ."

Scaring someone:
"You'd better do what I say."

Teasing or putting someone down:
"I can't believe you don't know that!"

Leaving someone out:
"You can't play," or
"You can't be in our club."

Embarrassing someone:
"Hey, everyone, watch this."

Spot the Difference

The best way to tell if you are being bullied is simply how it feels. Bullying is something done over and over, it's done on purpose, and it's meant to be hurtful. Being bullied feels bad. If it doesn't feel this way, it's not bullying.

(One says, "Sorry to bother you." The other says, "Move it!")

(One is complimenting the shirt. The other is making fun of it.)

BIG IMPORTANT POINT

Bullying isn't always about the words you use. It's *how* you say them that can cause a person to feel bullied. Think about where your words are coming from and how your attitude might affect someone else. Watch your body language and tone of voice. Before you speak, use your head—and your heart.

Why People Bully

Why on earth would someone want to hurt someone else?
Good question.

Maybe she . . .

- is lonely.
- is sad.
- is angry.
- has problems she doesn't know how to fix.
- is confusing being a leader with being a bully.
- is getting bullied at home.

- needs more attention.
- isn't very confident.
- is used to bullying others at home.
- doesn't realize that being hurtful is wrong.
- is trying to fit in.
- is jealous of other people's happiness.

Any of these could be the reason a girl chooses to bully others. Most often, a bully doesn't feel good about herself deep down. But hurting others is not the way to feel better. In fact, being a bully makes a person feel worse because at the end of the day, a person who bullies others can't really be proud of the person she is.

One thing is for sure . . .

When this boy in my class tries to shock me with scary talk, I feel upset inside. Sometimes it makes me sick to my stomach, and I have to leave class. It makes me feel like I have no strength. Then I just feel bad about myself.

A girl on my bus keeps teasing me. Yesterday she called my name, and when I turned around, she made a face at me and smiled a satisfied smile. Everyone around her laughed and smiled, too. When I got off the bus, I cried all the way home. I felt like I was all alone.

There is a girl who thinks she is queen. My two friends are her followers. She won't let them play with me or let me play with them. I can't understand why, and I feel so sad. I want to cry, and it makes it hard to pay attention in school. I just wish they could stand up to her and tell her she is being selfish and mean.

At my school and on my bus, a boy is bullying me. He is also mean to many other people. I am afraid to stand up to him because he always comes up with something to say to make me be quiet. I don't know what to do. I'm confused and a little scared.

Standing Up for Yourself

There is no one right way to deal with bullying. What may feel right for one person may not for another. What's important, though, is that you look at what's happening, what you've tried so far, and what your options are. Then figure out a plan and decide who can help you along the way.

Just Ignore It

Many times girls are told to just ignore a bully. True enough, sometimes ignoring works. Other times, it doesn't, and the bullying continues. Ignoring works best if you follow these tips.

Think fast

If ignoring is going to work, it will work fast. If you have tried ignoring and the bullying continues for several days or more, chances are it's not going to work. You need a new plan.

Look the part

When you are ignoring a bully, do your best to look bored or annoyed—not scared and especially not hurt. The bully is trying to upset you. Don't show that you're upset. Practice your best bored face at home, in front of a mirror.

Assess your stress

Are you thinking about the bullying all the time? If ignoring a bully is affecting your happiness most days, causing you to feel sad or worried, it's not worth it. Remember: you're not in the wrong here, and it's absolutely O.K. to stand up for yourself. Ignoring a bully is one option, but there are many others you can try.

How to Speak Up

Girls have lots of reasons for not standing up for themselves. But staying quiet doesn't always work, and getting in someone's face or talking behind her back isn't the answer. There's a better way.

It's called being *assertive*, or speaking up. It's the halfway point between being a pushover and being a bully. Here's how it works: you let the person know that you are not O.K. with the bullying, but you do it in a way that isn't mean and doesn't keep the fighting going.

Will one of these work for you? Practice a few clever comebacks at home so that you will be able to stand up for yourself when you need to.

☐ Tell it like it is. Try, "I don't like it when . . ."

☐ Simply disagree. Say, "I don't think so."

☐ Act surprised. Try, "I can't believe you just said that!"

☐ Let her have her point of view. Say, "That's your opinion."

☐ Ask a question, such as, "Was that really necessary? Really?"

☐ Use the one-word technique: "Wow."

☐ Question what she said. Try, "That doesn't even make sense."

☐ Use humor. Say, "Really? Thanks! That's just what I was trying for."

☐ Look confused. Just say, "What?" (Say this over and over if you need to.)

☐ Say her name: "Monica!"

BIG IMPORTANT POINT

None of these comebacks contain words that can get you into trouble with grown-ups. You have a right to defend yourself, and there are smart ways to do it. Just be sure you speak up in a way that solves problems and doesn't create more.

What's Your Speak-Up Style?

Do you stand up for yourself? How? Read each question, and circle the response that sounds most like you.

1. A boy trips and drops his lunch tray. You try to help, and a girl grabs your arm and tells you not to. You . . .

   a. stay seated, but you give the boy a kind look.

   b. pull your arm away and say to her, "Someone has to help him. I'd help if it were you."

   c. say to her, "What's your problem? You're so mean!"

2. A girl in your class tells all the girls except one to wear pink on Wednesday. You . . .

   a. feel bad for the girl who was left out, but you mind your own business.

   b. decide that you don't want to be a part of hurting someone's feelings. You skip the pink.

   c. secretly try to convince the girls to wear purple instead. That way the "rule maker" will feel left out.

3. While you're waiting in the lunch line, a classmate comes up, gives you a dirty look, and cuts in front of you. You . . .

a. do nothing. It's not worth it.

b. say, "You could've asked. I would've let you in."

c. say, "Hey, jerk! What do you think you're doing?!"

4. A girl on the playground asks you a personal question. You don't trust her. You respond by saying . . .

a. "I dunno," and make a quick exit.

b. "I'm not sure why you're asking me this. It's pretty personal, don't you think?"

c. "That's none of your business. I wouldn't tell you even if we *were* friends."

5. Every Friday is popcorn day at school. A girl in your class always expects you to give her money to get a bag of popcorn. You say . . .

a. nothing. After all, you started this by sharing with her in the first place, and you don't want to hurt her feelings.

b. "I wanted to give you the heads-up that I don't have extra money this week."

c. "I'm tired of you using me. Don't you have your own money?"

6. Some kids on the bus are picking on a boy from your neighborhood. You . . .

   a. feel bad for him and give him a smile when he passes by.

   b. invite him to sit with you.

   c. stand up and say, "Knock it off, you guys. Just because you're flunking out doesn't mean you have to pick on the smart kid!"

7. Two girls in your class are looking at you, whispering and giggling. You know they are making fun of you. You . . .

   a. show them how hurt you feel, but you say nothing.

   b. raise your eyebrows and say confidently, "C'mon, guys. Is that necessary?"

   c. walk right up to them and say, "What's the matter? Are you too scared to say that to my face?"

8. Puppies are your absolutely most favorite thing in the world. Everyone knows it. One day, a girl in your class forms a "puppy club," but she says you can't join. You . . .

   a. shrug your shoulders and find someone else to play with.

   b. say, "That's O.K. Clubs like that don't really work for me anyway."

   c. say, "No problem. I'll start my own club and invite everyone but *you*."

26

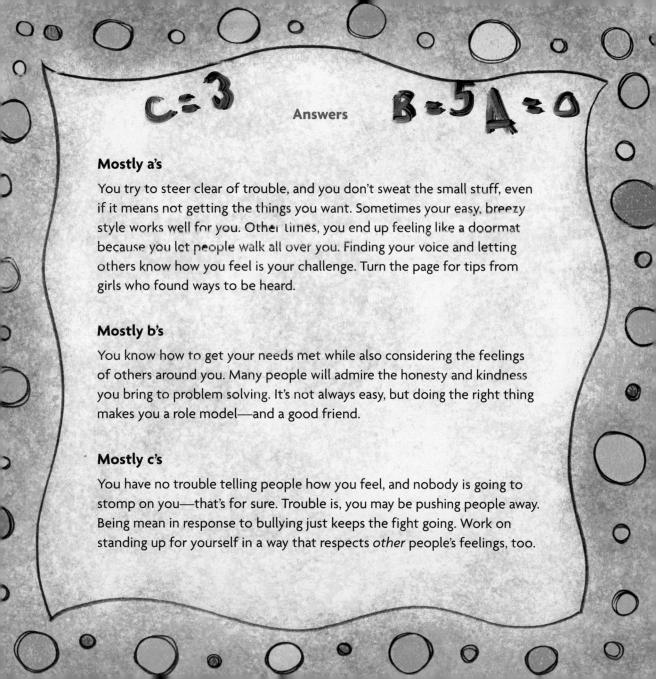

C = 3

Answers

B = 5 A = 0

Mostly a's

You try to steer clear of trouble, and you don't sweat the small stuff, even if it means not getting the things you want. Sometimes your easy, breezy style works well for you. Other times, you end up feeling like a doormat because you let people walk all over you. Finding your voice and letting others know how you feel is your challenge. Turn the page for tips from girls who found ways to be heard.

Mostly b's

You know how to get your needs met while also considering the feelings of others around you. Many people will admire the honesty and kindness you bring to problem solving. It's not always easy, but doing the right thing makes you a role model—and a good friend.

Mostly c's

You have no trouble telling people how you feel, and nobody is going to stomp on you—that's for sure. Trouble is, you may be pushing people away. Being mean in response to bullying just keeps the fight going. Work on standing up for yourself in a way that respects *other* people's feelings, too.

Words That Work

Need more inspiration to speak up? Try these tips from girls like you.

I say, "Oh, well!" If that's the way they want to be, let them be that way. It's their problem.

I just say, "Thanks, but I'm good," and then I walk away.

I just say, "Right back atcha!" and get away from them.

29

Staying Strong at School

Being bullied at school is the worst. How can you concentrate when you're being picked on? Kids who bully are looking for a reaction. If you look upset, you'll be giving them the reaction they want. Instead, follow these tips to look strong and stand tall.

Act confident

Hold your head high and your shoulders back. Look the person in the eye, and try to keep your voice steady while you are talking. Acting confident will help you *feel* more confident.

Take a break

If you feel your confidence fading, step away from the situation and give yourself a pep talk.

Keep it cool

Try to look annoyed or bored. Don't let the bully know she's gotten to you.

Splash!

If you feel as if your insides are on fire, cool down with a large drink of water. Or splash water on your face to help calm those hot feelings.

Breathe

Take a few long, deep breaths. Breathe in confidence and strength, and breathe out your stress and worry.

Let it out

Think about an adult at school who can listen and help if you're having a tough day. If you don't have someone at school, write your feelings down so that you can talk about them when you get home.

Here's what NOT to do:

- Don't threaten things you are not willing to follow through on.
- Don't try to get even. Two wrongs don't make a right.
- Don't ask others to take sides. That will just keep the fight going.
- Don't stay home from school to avoid the bully.
- Don't get hysterical—avoid yelling, whining, and losing control.

What If It's Not Working?

You've tried ignoring the bully and you've tried standing up for yourself, but the bully isn't backing down. If this is happening to you, take heart. It's not easy to stand strong, but there *is* another option right around the corner.

Step 1: Reach out

Many girls feel embarrassed about being bullied. Just remember that it's NOT your fault. If you've tried speaking up and that's not working, get help from a parent or another adult you trust. Talk about what you have tried so far, and come up with a new plan that you are both comfortable with.

Step 2: Keep track

Start writing down when and where the bullying happens. Add a note about how you handle the bullying, too.

Step 3: Heads up!

Let your teacher in on what's up and what you have tried so far. She can keep an eye out for the bullying and maybe catch it while it's happening.

Step 4: Give a warning

Say firmly to the bully, "Leave me alone or I'll report you," or "This is bullying and you need to stop." That's enough to send the message that you mean business. Caution: If the bullying is severe and you feel unsafe, don't wait. Go straight to step 5.

Step 5: Enough is enough

If you've given the bully fair warning and the bullying continues, it's time to make a full report to the teacher or principal. Ask your parents to go with you, and take the notes you've written.

Getting Support

Now is the time to take extra care of yourself and to feel the support of those closest to you. Remember: a bully is trying to take your power. Hang on to it by reaching out to your family and doing things that make you feel strong, confident, and loved.

Keep talking

Talk regularly to your parents about what's happening. Set aside time to share your feelings, and work together to find a solution. You don't need to go through this alone.

Show team spirit

Your siblings can help, too. Hold a family meeting, and brainstorm ways for you to deal with the bully. *Role-play*, or act out, different responses. If you're the oldest, you'll be teaching your siblings how to stand up for themselves. If you have older siblings who have been there, you can learn from their experiences.

Pour on the fun

When school is stressful, make sure that life at home isn't. Plan fun things during your free time. Cook or bake, have a family game night, read a great book, watch an inspiring movie, take a bubble bath, write in your journal, or call a faraway relative or friend. Try lots of different ways to lift your spirits.

Powerful Reminders

A *motto* is a positive saying that reminds you of who you are and what you are about. When you repeat your motto to yourself, negative feelings fade away. It doesn't matter what anyone else says about you, because you know better. These tokens will remind you of your motto when you need it most.

Beads of bravery

Make a bracelet or key chain out of beads that spell out the first letter of each word in your motto. If your motto is **"I'm strong, smart, and totally amazing,"** string beads with the letters **I, S, S, T,** and **A**. Wear the bracelet or tuck it into your pocket. When you feel the wave of sadness that comes with being bullied, think of the motto and touch the beads to give yourself strength and confidence.

Solid as a rock

Use a permanent marker to write the initials of your motto on a small, smooth rock. Carry the rock with you throughout the day.

Daily doodles

Write the initials of your motto on your notebook cover, on a postcard that you stick in your locker, or on a scrap of paper that you tuck into your pocket.

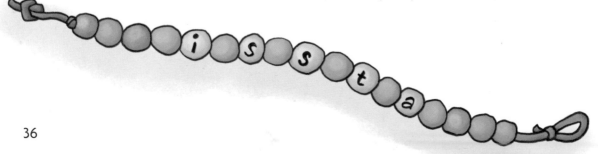

Where else can you find strength? Look no further than your closet or your CD collection.

Colorful clothing

Does the color red make you feel strong? Then layer it on. Wear a red T-shirt on the days you need extra courage, or give yourself small bursts of bravery with a red headband, a bracelet, or painted toenails.

Feel-good music

Find the songs that speak to you, and put them all on a CD or playlist. When you don't have your stereo or MP3 player with you, hum a few lines of a song in your head until you feel better.

Box of inspiration

Decorate a shoe box, and fill it with notes, poems, quotes, and photos that make you feel good about who you are. Keep adding to the box, and pull it out when you need a boost.

What Do You Do?

The lunch supervisor at school seems to have something against you. She makes comments on what you pack, how fast you eat, and even how you laugh! You don't know why she doesn't like you, but it's obvious she doesn't, and it's getting harder every day.

It's true—adults can bully, too. And being bullied by an adult can be especially painful and confusing. Whether that bully is a troop leader, a teacher, or a coach, you need to ask for help from another adult you trust. This takes a LOT of courage. Write down what is happening at lunch, and keep talking with another adult about how best to handle the situation. Remember that no one deserves to be bullied, whether by a kid or by an adult. It's just not O.K., ever.

You did it again. Whenever you're around Mimi, the "queen bee" in your class, you say something to annoy her, and she ends up humiliating you in front of her friends. You know you're making things worse by talking to her, but you do it anyway. How can you slow down and stop yourself?

Maybe you open your mouth because you're nervous, or maybe you're trying to stick up for yourself because Mimi has hurt your feelings in the past. Either way, saying whatever is on your mind to a person like Mimi is fueling her fire. It may be best to try to avoid her altogether. If you see her and you feel the urge to say something, write it down first. When you see it in writing, you'll know whether it's something to share or not.

You're talking to Marti on the computer, and she starts saying mean things—*really* mean things—about Sarah. You can't believe what you're reading, and you're not sure what to do. Is this bullying?

You bet. It's called *cyberbullying,* and it's serious. Cyberbullying is using the Internet or cell phones to embarrass or hurt someone. If a friend starts bad-mouthing another friend on-line, you have options. You can say "gotta go" and log off. You can change the subject and hope she gets the hint. Or you can tell your friend straight up, "I don't want to talk about Sarah. She's my friend, just as you are. I would never let someone talk about you that way." If you ever receive a mean message directed at YOU, don't respond. Log off, and let your parents know right away. They can help you decide how to handle the situation. And when you're writing a message to someone? Always think before pressing the "send" button, especially if you're angry. Once you put something in writing, you can't take it back.

Girls Who Stood Strong

If you are being bullied, you're not alone.
Many girls have gone through the same thing.

My bully troubles started in fifth grade at a new school. A girl started teasing me. She spread terrible rumors about me. She made fun of my body and my clothing, too. I tried to do what my family said and just ignore her, but I couldn't take it. I waited for a time when lots of teachers were around, and then I said straight to her face, "Stop saying mean things that aren't true! If you want me to go to the teachers, you can just keep spreading rumors!" She gave me nasty looks for the rest of the year, but I didn't care. At least she stopped making up things about me.

My friend Brittany would be nice some days and mean other days. I started to get stomach aches and couldn't sleep because I was worried about whether she'd ever be my friend again. I finally learned that if Brittany wanted to be mean, I would have to pull away and open up to other girls— stronger girls. I learned that you can control your own life.

There was a boy in my class who used to say AWFUL things to me. He would say anything to get me upset, and it got so bad that I didn't want to go to school. I would get sick a lot and couldn't get my work done. I was very unhappy. My mom and I let the teacher know, and she tried to help by watching what was happening. She also checked in with me, which helped a LOT. In the end, I stood up to him by making a joke and pretending I didn't care what he said. I felt stronger after that. Looking back, I'm not even sure why I was so scared of him!

Standing Up for Others

When you see someone being bullied, you have an important choice to make. You can stand around and watch, or you can stand up for that person. If you stand up for her, you'll feel great— and you might add to the list of people who will be there for you if you ever need them.

Being a Good Bystander

That is so mean. How could you say that?

A person who sees someone else being bullied is called a *bystander*. One way to be a good bystander is to say out loud to the bully that you don't agree with her and you want her to stop. Can't find the words? Practice a few of these.

"Leave her alone."

"It's not a joke unless everyone is laughing."

"Wow. That's just wrong."

"C'mon, let's get out of here!"

"Stop it!"

Telling vs. Tattling

Another way to be a good bystander is to report what is happening to an adult. Afraid of being a tattletale? You won't be. There's a HUGE difference between telling and tattling. Knowing the difference will give you the courage and confidence to report bullying when you see it.

Tattling

You're trying to **make someone look bad.** The goal is not to help someone but to get someone into trouble.

Telling

You're reporting a behavior that is hurting you or someone else. It's something you feel adults should know about, and you *are* trying to **help someone.** Chances are, you're not the only one who doesn't like what's going on. If you speak up, others may, too.

Ways to report

You can . . .

- visit the school counselor.
- deliver an anonymous note to a teacher or to the principal.
- sit down with a parent and write a note or e-mail together.
- ask a parent to talk to school officials without you—that's perfectly O.K.

Just **do something.** By reporting bullying, you give the people in charge the chance to do something about it.

47

Girls Who Stood Up for Others

Here's how other girls found the courage to be good bystanders:

There is a kid who said really bad things to my friends. I stood up for them by saying, "EWWWW, that's gross! Keep your thoughts to yourself." I'm not sure if he got into trouble, but he hasn't done it since. If he does it again, I'll report it, because that's just wrong.

Once I heard a boy in my class make really rude comments to a girl on the playground. The girl looked upset by what he was saying, and I knew it was wrong but wasn't sure what to do. That night, I told my mom. She said I was right to tell her, and together, we wrote an e-mail to the teacher. No one ever knew that I was the one who stood up for that girl, but I knew, and it made me feel really good.

Last year, my three new "friends" were ganging up on one girl who had a problem with her speech. I felt horrible, but it was REALLY hard to go against my friends. But I asked myself, "If they are pressuring me to do things I don't want to do, are they really my friends?"

The answer is no. If they threaten to take away their friendship, their friendship isn't worth that much. Being nice to someone who is being bullied gives you confidence in yourself—and more power than any bully has.

One day my friends were being really mean to a girl who gets picked on, and I joined in. When I got home I felt really bad, so I called the girl and told her I was sorry. She really appreciated that I called her. Now when kids are teasing her, I stand up for her. Once I started standing up for this girl, many other girls started doing the same.

Caring for Friends

Speaking up isn't always easy, and sometimes the chance to be a good bystander passes you by. But it's never too late to let a friend know you're in her corner.

Say what you think

Say, "They're wrong," or "They're bullies. Don't listen to them." Try, "I think you're a great person," "That was not cool," or simply "Hang in there."

Send her a note

A little bit of kindness can go a long way. Write, "Sending a smile your way" or "Ten things I like about you."

Help her reach out

Offer to go with her to report what is happening, or encourage her to talk to an adult.

Make a wish

Tell her what you wish could've happened or what you wish you had said or done.

Stick up for her

Reassure her that you won't take part in any gossip behind her back. Tell her that you would never do that—and then don't.

Stay close

Give her a hug, sit by her at lunch, and stand by her in gym. Just having you close will mean a lot.

Give her a break

Call her, tell her a joke, or make plans to get together outside of school. Don't waste your time talking about the negative stuff at school. Instead, focus on having fun.

What Do You Stand For?

It's easier to stand up for yourself and others when you know what you believe. Read each statement below and decide whether you agree or disagree. Check off your choice.

1. One student like me can't really make my school a better place.

   ☐ **agree**   ✓ disagree

2. If I try hard enough, I can keep everyone happy.

   ☐ **agree**   ✓ disagree

3. When someone makes me angry, it's O.K. for me to be mean.

   ☐ **agree**   ✓ disagree

4. It's easiest to go along with my friends, even when something they're doing doesn't feel quite right.

   ☐ **agree**   ✓ disagree

5. People who act "different" are sort of asking to be bullied.

   ☐ **agree**   ✓ disagree

6. If I'm upset with a friend, it's probably time to end the friendship.

   ☐ **agree**   ✓ disagree

Answers

Did you check "disagree" most often? If so, you know how to stand up for your beliefs—and how to respect other people's points of view. It's not easy to do both. These tips should help:

1. The principal isn't the only one with power at your school. Every time you give a kind smile or help someone out, you make your school a better place. One person can make a difference, and you're just the one to do it.

2. It's impossible to keep everyone happy all the time. If you tried, you'd never sleep (and it wouldn't work!). What matters is staying true to yourself so that you can be proud of who you are.

3. It's O.K. to be angry. You can't control how you feel, but you *can* control how you respond. Being mean almost always makes things worse. Next time you feel angry, slow down and think about why you feel that way. Then figure out the best way to deal with it.

4. It may seem easiest to give in to peer pressure. But you have to live with your decisions, and there's nothing easy about knowing that you did something you knew was wrong. Listen to the voice inside of you *before* doing something you'll regret.

5. No one should be bullied for being different. In some ways, we are *all* different. And it's our differences that make us interesting! Stand up for those who are different, because the world would be a boring place without them.

6. Nobody's perfect. You're not, and your friends aren't either. Making mistakes is part of being human, so try to give friends a chance to make things right. But if a friend *keeps* doing things that are hurtful, it's time to set some limits.

Changing Friendships

Does standing up for what you believe sometimes mean clashing with friends? Absolutely. Friends can disagree—that's O.K. But if it seems as if you just can't get along, take time to figure out why.

Talk to your friend

If you think a friendship is worth fighting for, have a heart-to-heart talk with your friend. Tell her how you are feeling, and then decide if you can work things out. You may have to agree to disagree on some things.

Stay open

Part of growing up is making mistakes (and forgiving them). Never be too proud to apologize or too stubborn to accept an apology.

Watch and wait

Maybe there is something going on with your friend, or maybe she's just trying on different roles. Put off making big decisions and see what happens. This problem may be temporary.

Focus on other friends

If you and your friend are moving in different directions, it's O.K. You can still be friends. You just might spend less time together. Be friendly and kind, and put energy into other relationships that allow you to be YOU. You deserve that!

BIG IMPORTANT POINT

Not all friendships will last a lifetime. In fact, that's very rare. Over time, some of your friendships will deepen, and some will slip away. Don't be afraid of changing friendships. They allow you to change and grow, too.

What Do You Do?

You made a mistake. You shared a secret that you shouldn't have, and now your friend Cierra can barely look at you. You've really hurt her feelings, and you feel terrible. What do you do?

You try to make it right. Admitting you were wrong isn't easy. But taking responsibility for your mistakes is the first step toward healing the damage. Apologize to your friend. Tell her what you wish you had done and what you'll do differently in the future. Be sensitive, and be patient. In time, she may forgive you. If she doesn't, you'll know you've done all you can—and learned a difficult lesson about the importance of trust in a friendship.

Melani used to make fun of you in second grade. In fact, you still get a sick feeling in your stomach when you think about it. Now she wants to be your friend. Can you ever forgive her?

If you believe she is truly sorry for hurting you and wants to be friends, then you may want to give it a try. That doesn't mean you have to be close friends right away, or ever. Just give her a chance to earn back your respect and friendship. Take it slowly. Don't accept the "best friends" necklace from Melani just yet, and wait before doing an overnight or spending lots of one-on-one time with her. After a while you'll know if you can be good friends or if you're better off as casual pals.

You're on the playground, and you notice Alex picking on your friend Leigh. He won't let her shoot a basket, and she looks frustrated. You want to stand up for her, but you're not sure she wants you to. Should you step in, or wait and see what happens?

Good question. You should step in only if it looks as if Leigh can't stand up for herself. If you're not sure whether she can or she can't, just ask her if she's O.K. Even if she is only playing around with Alex, she'll appreciate your concern. But remember: if it looks as if Leigh is being hurt physically or is being bullied by several people at a time, tell an adult right away.

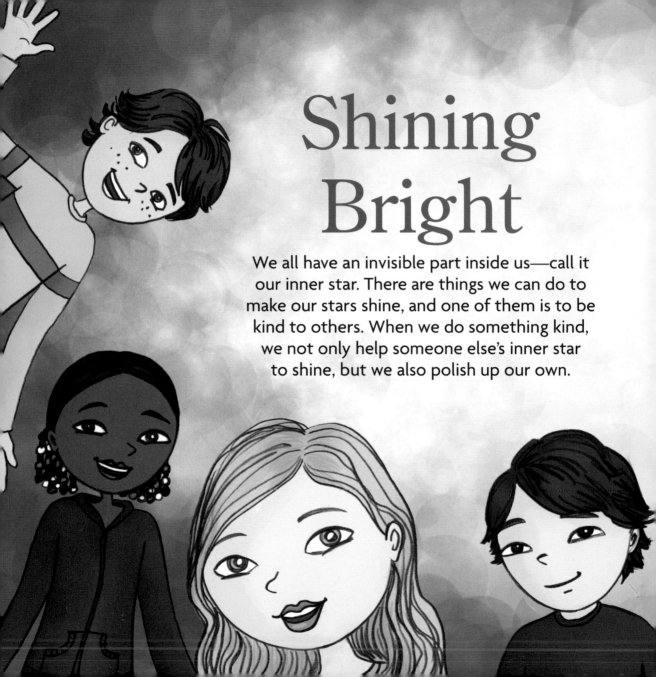

Shining Bright

We all have an invisible part inside us—call it our inner star. There are things we can do to make our stars shine, and one of them is to be kind to others. When we do something kind, we not only help someone else's inner star to shine, but we also polish up our own.

Whenever you can, help other people shine.

Give second chances.

Give a warm smile.

Laugh at other people's jokes.

Offer a compliment.

Stand up for them when
they need it most.

Send a kind note.

Apologize—and mean it.

Give a hug.

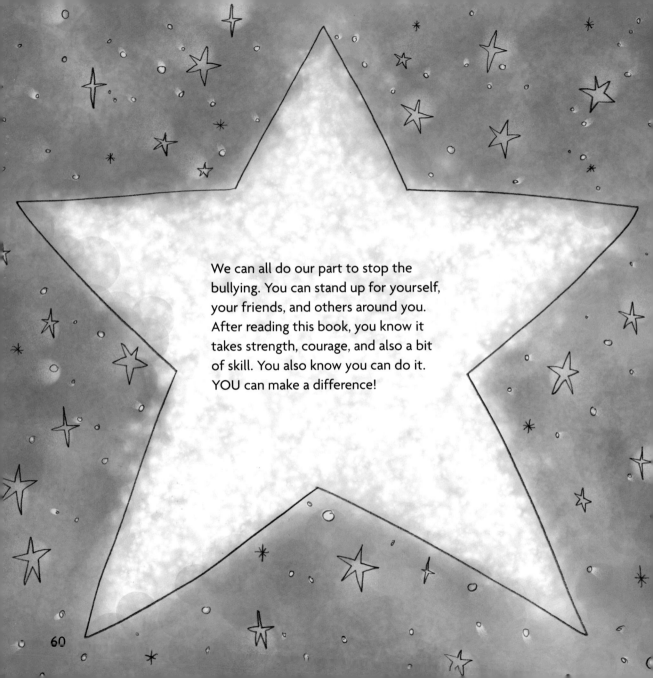

We can all do our part to stop the bullying. You can stand up for yourself, your friends, and others around you. After reading this book, you know it takes strength, courage, and also a bit of skill. You also know you can do it. YOU can make a difference!

Make a promise to yourself that you'll stand up when you need to. Cut out this promise and hang it on your mirror or on the back of your bedroom door—anywhere you'll see it often, remember it, and feel the power of its words.

I, _____ , will

Print your name here.

S tand up to put-downs,

H elp those who are being bullied,

I nform adults when I need to,

N ever use my computer or cell phone to hurt others, and

E ncourage my friends to stand up against bullying, too.

I promise to stand strong, speak out, and be a good friend. I will let my inner star shine!

Name: _____

Write your signature here.

Date: _____3-2-12_____

Write to us!
Tell us how you stood up for yourself
or for someone else. Send letters to:

Stand Up for Yourself Editor
American Girl
8400 Fairway Place
Middleton, WI 53562

Photos can't be returned. All comments and suggestions
received by American Girl may be used without
compensation or acknowledgment.

Also from American Girl:

Chrissa Maxwell has just moved to town and can't wait to make friends at her new school. She starts school on Valentine's Day and has a rude awakening when three mean girls in her class decide to make her life miserable. Read Chrissa's stories and find out how she learns to stand up to the bullies.

"Didn't get any valentines?" Tara whispered. "How sad!"

And then Sonali and Jadyn started giggling.

I sat up straight, too upset to speak. I didn't want to jump to any conclusions. It was possible that I had received only one valentine, but my gut told me they had been stolen.

—from *Chrissa*, by Mary Casanova

Chrissa's stories also come to life on DVD!

Remember: Talking to a parent or another adult you trust can help you stand up to bullying. Here's something else to share with the grown-ups in your life. Pull it out and pass it on!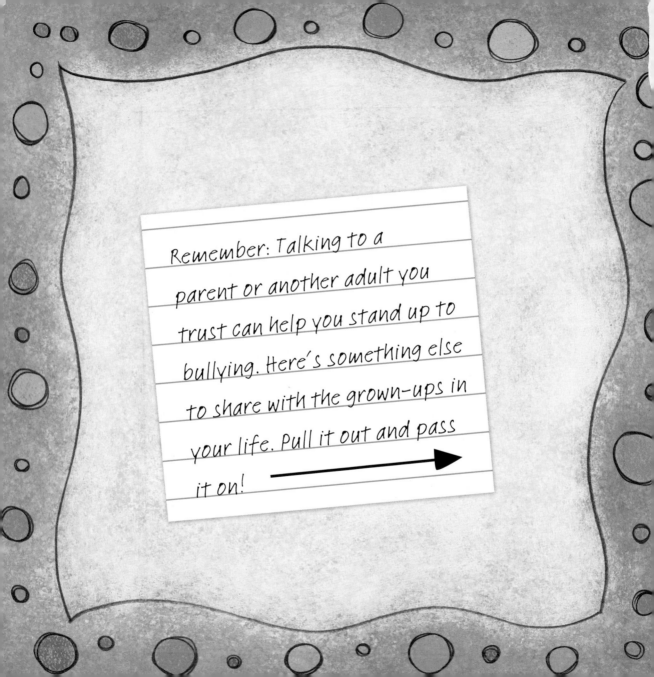